KS2 SATs Practice Papers

10-Minute English Grammar, Punctuation & Spelling Tests for Year 6

Book II

Ages 10-11

2020-2021 Edition

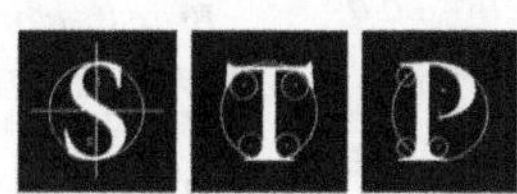

This book contains **18 bite-size 10-Minute Grammar, Punctuation and Spelling Tests** designed for **Year 6** students.

Divided into 3 groups, each group is full of **realistic practice for Paper 1 and Paper 2** of the KS2 SATs English examinations, written in line with the new testing requirements.

Each **test** is made up of **10 questions**. Each question is worth 1 mark.

Students should try to complete each test within **10 minutes**.

At the start of the book, students will find **Notes** explaining how to do the 10-minute tests.

At the end of the book, parents and teachers will find

- **Complete Answers**
- **Guidelines** for marking the **Grammar & Punctuation Tests**
- Brief, clear instructions for **Administering & Marking the Spelling Tests**
- The **Spelling Test Transcripts** which are to be read aloud to students.

Before you get started...

This book comes with FREE printable Self-Assessment Sheets & a Test Diary for students.

To access them, simply visit our website @ https://bit.ly/3kFYvWa or use the QR code below:

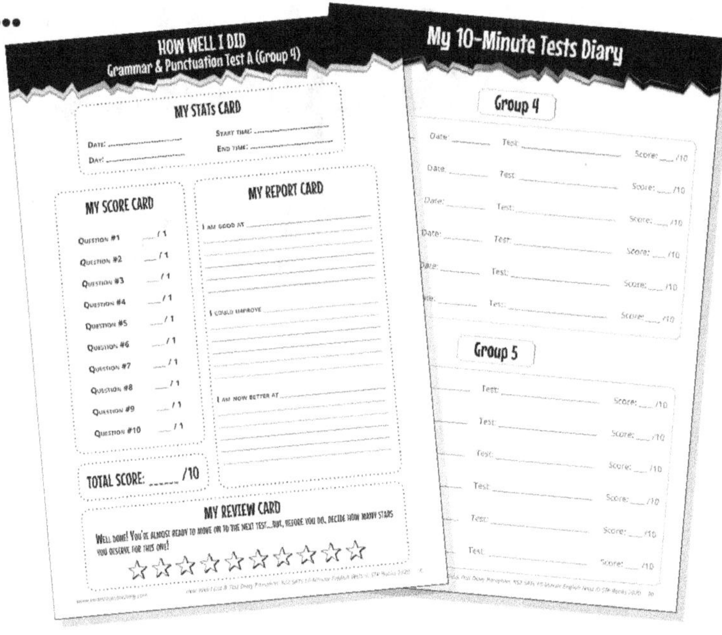

Published by STP Books
An imprint of Swot Tots Publishing Ltd
Kemp House
152-160 City Road
London EC1V 2NX

www.swottotspublishing.com

Typeset, cover design, and inside concept design by Swot Tots Publishing Ltd.

British Library Cataloguing-in-Publication Data. A catalogue record for this book is available from the British Library.

ISBN 978-1-912956-24-1

CONTENTS

Notes for Students

DOING THE GRAMMAR & PUNCTUATION TESTS

- Each Grammar and Punctuation Test is made up of 10 different types of questions for you to answer in different ways.
- Each question heading will make it clear to you what kind of answer is needed e.g. ticking a box, circling a word, writing a short answer.
- Each correct answer is worth 1 mark.
- You should try to complete each test within 10 MINUTES.

DOING THE SPELLING TESTS

- Each Spelling Test is made up of 10 sentences.
- In each sentence, there is a BLANK SPACE for you to fill in with the ONE WORD that is MISSING from the sentence.
- You will need to get someone to READ OUT the missing words for you from the transcripts in this book.
- You should try to complete each test within 10 MINUTES.

DON'T FORGET....

You can download your FREE printable 10-MINUTE TEST DIARY and HOW WELL I DID pamphlet for all the tests in this book from our website.

Either visit us @ http://bit.ly/3kFYvWa or, you can use the following QR code:

Good Luck!

1.   **Tick ONE BOX** to show which sentence should end with an **exclamation mark**.

Wash in cold water before wearing for the first time ☐

The women all looked very glamorous in their evening dresses ☐

How pretty she looked in that gown ☐

Did you see Jasper in his dinner jacket ☐

1 mark

2.   Insert a **dash** in the correct place in the following sentence.

There   is   only   one   solution   to   the   problem   work.

1 mark

3.   **Tick ONE BOX** to show which sentence uses **capital letters** correctly.

Last Tuesday, at the theatre, we saw a shakespeare Play: *Hamlet*. ☐

Last Tuesday, at the theatre, we saw a Shakespeare play: *Hamlet***.** ☐

Last tuesday, at the theatre, we saw a Shakespeare play: *Hamlet*. ☐

last Tuesday, at the theatre, we saw a Shakespeare play: *Hamlet*. ☐

1 mark

4.   The **prefix** <u>bi-</u> can be used with the word <u>annual</u> to make the word <u>biannual</u>. **Tick ONE BOX** to show what the word **biannual** means.

every year ☐

every two years ☐

twice every other year ☐

twice a year ☐

1 mark

5.   **Tick ONE BOX** to show which **verb form** completes the sentence below correctly.

The bookshelves are much tidier now that Maria _______ them.

had organised ☐

has organised ☐

was organised ☐

are organising ☐

1 mark

5

6.   Circle the correct **verb form** in each underlined pair to complete the following sentences.

It **don't / doesn't** feel very warm today.

Sue and Francis **don't / doesn't** believe in ghosts.

Nolan argued that we **don't / doesn't** need to keep buying lots of unnecessary things.   1 mark

7.   **Tick ONE BOX** to show which option completes the sentence below correctly.

_______________________________ to warn them of the danger.

As fast as possible, Raymond raced ☐

As fast as possible Raymond raced, ☐

As fast as possible Raymond, raced ☐

As fast as, possible Raymond raced ☐   1 mark

8.   **Tick ONE BOX** to show which sentence is correctly punctuated.

I want to read a book, watch TV, listen to music, and go swimming at the same time. ☐

I want to read a book, watch TV, listen to music and, go swimming at the same time. ☐

I want to read a book, watch TV listen to music and go swimming at the same time. ☐

I want to read a book, watch TV, listen to music and go swimming at the same time. ☐   1 mark

9.   **Tick ONE BOX** to show the **word class** of the underlined word in the sentence below.

You'd better hurry up and eat that ice cream <u>before</u> it melts!

conjunction ☐

adverb ☐

preposition ☐

adjective ☐   1 mark

10.   **Tick ONE BOX** to show the correct place for a **semi-colon** in the following sentence.

The doorbell rang we all looked at each other in great surprise.
☐ ☐   ☐   ☐   1 mark

End of Test A! Now check your answers on p. 38!

1.   **Tick ONE BOX** to show the **word class** of the underlined words in the sentence below.

The girl who <u>is</u> standing by the gates <u>has</u> <u>been</u> elected to the student council.

adverbs ☐

nouns ☐

verbs ☐

adjectives ☐

1 mark

2.   **Tick ONE BOX** to show which sentence is correctly punctuated.

I like the idea of: a hybrid a car that uses both petrol and electricity. ☐

I like the idea of a hybrid: a car that uses both petrol and electricity. ☐

I like the idea of a hybrid a car that uses: both petrol and electricity. ☐

I like the idea of a hybrid a car that uses both: petrol and electricity. ☐

1 mark

3.   **Tick ONE BOX** to show which sentence uses the word <u>before</u> as a **preposition**.

<u>Before</u> you go to bed, make sure you turn off the lights. ☐

Something must be done about this <u>before</u> it's too late! ☐

Eric made several phone calls <u>before</u> he left the office. ☐

Doing it this way is like putting the cart <u>before</u> the horse. ☐

1 mark

4.   **Tick ONE BOX** to show which sentence is correctly punctuated.

Betty, much to her surprise has won, this month's competition. ☐

Betty, much to her surprise, has won this month's competition. ☐

Betty much to her surprise has won, this month's, competition. ☐

Betty much, to her surprise, has won this month's competition. ☐

1 mark

5.   Complete the sentence below with an appropriate **co-ordinating conjunction**.

There's no use crying, _______________________ the opportunity is gone.

1 mark

7

6. **Tick ONE BOX** to show which sentence is a **question**.

Have everything collected by tomorrow afternoon ☐

What is left to collect from the shed is negligible ☐

Have you collected all your things from the hall ☐

Who collected all this rubbish is a mystery ☐

1 mark

---

7. **Tick ONE BOX** to show which sentence uses the word <u>clean</u> as a **verb**.

<u>Clean</u> your teeth properly after every meal. ☐

As her parents were visiting, Jackie gave the flat a good <u>clean</u>. ☐

Having a <u>clean</u> driving licence would help you get the job. ☐

Cinderella was amazed; the dirty clothes had been washed <u>clean</u>! ☐

1 mark

---

8. **Tick ONE BOX** to show which sentence uses **capital letters** correctly.

Yolanda travelled to a South Pacific island last year. ☐

The School Play is being performed next week. ☐

The winner of the nobel Peace Prize has been announced. ☐

The local Bakery will close this coming February. ☐

1 mark

---

9. Insert a **pair of commas** in the correct place in the sentence below.

War Horse a novel written by Michael Morpurgo and which is set in World War I has been made into both a film and a play.

1 mark

---

10. Replace the underlined words in the sentences below with the correct **pronouns**.

"Look at those girls!" said the twins excitedly. "The raincoats <u>the girls</u> are wearing have the same patterns as <u>the raincoats that belong to us</u>!"

1 mark

End of Test B! Now check your answers on p. 38!

1. **Tick ONE BOX** to show which sentence is punctuated correctly.

"Please be quiet" said Gina, "because the baby's asleep." ☐

"Please, be quiet," said Gina, "because the baby's asleep." ☐

"Please be quiet," said Gina, "because the baby's asleep." ☐

"Please, be quiet," said Gina "because the baby's asleep". ☐

1 mark

2. **Tick ONE BOX** to show which of the following sentences is the most **informal**.

The coach told us not to be late for rugby practice. ☐

"Lateness to rugby practice will not be tolerated," said the coach. ☐

Make sure you arrive on time for rugby practice. ☐

"Be on time for rugby practice, guys!" said the coach. ☐

1 mark

3. **Tick ONE BOX** to show which underlined words form a **main clause**.

<u>When we woke up</u>, we discovered that it had been snowing. ☐

We might go to the seaside <u>if the weather is good tomorrow</u>. ☐

Millie grated the carrots and <u>Peter mashed the potatoes</u>. ☐

Our local MP, <u>whose name I can't remember</u>, is a woman. ☐

1 mark

4. Circle the two words that are **antonyms** in the following sentence.

After the frightening storm had eased, the turbulent waves of the sea that had been so alarming gradually became more tranquil.

1 mark

5. **Tick ONE BOX** in each row to show if the apostrophe is used for **possession** or **contraction**.

SENTENCE	Possession	Contraction
Jade hid Fred's glasses.		
Where's the remote control?		
Their dog's gone missing.		
Omar can't come to the party.		

1 mark

6. **Tick ONE BOX** to show which sentence contains a **relative clause**.

The clock that is on the mantelpiece is an antique. ☐

I didn't think the meal was that nice. ☐

If Carl gets that job, he'll be thrilled. ☐

I think I will buy that red dress over there. ☐

1 mark

7. **Tick ONE BOX** to show which sentence below is a **statement**.

You aren't driving too fast, are you ☐

He was asked to drive slowly ☐

Use your indicators when driving ☐

How well am I driving ☐

1 mark

8. Insert **capital letters** and **full stops** in the passage below so that it is punctuated correctly.

Hussein is the best striker in our team he didn't play last Saturday because he'd hurt his knee and we lost we're hoping he'll be better next weekend

1 mark

9. Insert a **pair of dashes** in the correct place in the following sentence.

Expensive designer clothes especially those which are made in Italy are regularly to be seen in magazines.

1 mark

10. Complete the sentences below by rewriting the verbs in boxes in the correct **tense**.

Iris and Sean had _________________ their work by the time the bell rang.

| to complete |

The Great Pyramid of Giza's construction _________________ over 4,000 years ago.

| to begin |

1 mark

End of Test C! Now check your answers on p. 39!

1. Write a **command** which could be the first step in the instructions for using a washing machine. Make sure you punctuate your answer correctly.

____

1 mark

2. In the sentence below, identify each of the clauses as either **main (M)** or **subordinate (S)**.

Saladin, the pure-bred Arabian, streaked ahead of the other horses, so he won the race easily.

1 mark

3. Circle the **conjunction** in each of the following sentences.

Steve runs because he wants to lose a few pounds.

Lionel, my friend, jogs every day, yet he is still unfit.

Once Marissa has been for a run, she does her stretches.

1 mark

4. **Tick TWO BOXES** to show which sentences contain a **determiner**.

Rick passed an interesting-looking bookshop.

Utterly exhausted, Vera sat down and sighed heavily.

The distant mountainous horizon was forbidding.

Tomorrow, I shall travel north.

1 mark

5. **Tick ONE BOX** to identify the **subject** of the following sentence.

Had he studied French at school, Malcolm would have been given the job.

school

French

job

Malcolm

1 mark

11

6. Insert **two commas** and a **semi-colon** in the correct places in the following sentence.

Helen my favourite cousin enjoyed watching the latest Star Wars film she'd been looking forward to it ever since they'd announced it was being made. <u>1 mark</u>

7. Circle the **possessive pronoun** in the following sentence.

The Browns are having lunch at a favourite restaurant of theirs: a small Italian bistro which has been mentioned in the local newspaper as it's won several awards. <u>1 mark</u>

8. Rewrite the verbs in the boxes below using the **past simple tense** to complete the sentence.

There ___________________ a great deal of amusement at Charlie's expense yesterday when

to be

he ___________________ over his shoelaces and ___________________ into the paddling pool.

to trip		to fall

<u>1 mark</u>

9. Insert a **pair of brackets** in the correct place in the following sentence.

Yesterday, I saw that dog steal two sandwiches one beef and one turkey as well as several sausages from the butcher's. <u>1 mark</u>

10. Identify the one **prefix** which can be added to all three of the following words to make their antonyms. Write your answer in the box.

democratic
embarrassed
returnable

<u>1 mark</u>

End of Test D! Now check your answers on p. 39!

1. Circle the two words that are **synonyms** in the following passage.

Although the tiny elf was exceedingly timid, he was also perceptive. Indeed, it was evident to all that it had been his observant remarks that had prevented a disastrous war with the goblins.

1 mark

2. Circle the **relative pronoun** in the following sentence.

The teacher told me, "Your painting technique is as good as Harriet's whose picture won my art prize last year."

1 mark

3. **Tick ONE BOX** to show which **punctuation mark** should be in the place indicated by the arrow.

The solution to the mystery, which, as indeed Sherlock Holmes himself finally admitted was one that combined the bizarre with the mundane. ↑

dash ☐

hyphen ☐

comma ☐

semi-colon ☐

1 mark

4. Use a word formed from the root word <u>delight</u> to complete each of the sentences below.

"What a _______________________ surprise to see you!" said Maria, beaming.

The children clapped their hands _______________________ at the news.

1 mark

5. Use an **adjective** formed from the word <u>suffice</u> to complete the following sentence.

I think there is _______________________ petrol in the tank for us to get home.

1 mark

6. Insert **three hyphens** in the correct places in the following sentence.

Ashish has bought a state of the art computer which he will use for a lot of graphic design work along with editing videos and streaming music.

1 mark

7. Rewrite the sentence below in the **active voice**. Make sure you punctuate your answer correctly.

Severe flooding has been caused in some places by the heavy rain.

____

1 mark

8. Rewrite the verbs that are underlined in the following sentences so that they are in the **past progressive** form.

We <u>watched</u> the news on TV. The headlines <u>were</u> read out.

1 mark

9. Complete the following sentence using a **noun phrase** containing at least three words. Make sure you punctuate your answer correctly.

Screaming loudly, ____

________________________________tried to escape from the fire-breathing dragon.

1 mark

10. Circle the **adjective** in the following sentence.

"That's a likely story!" Bill harrumphed irritably in disbelief.

1 mark

End of Test E! Now check your answers on p. 39!

1. A large crack appeared in the ______________________________.   1 mark

2. Bella ______________________________ the right answer.   1 mark

3. The chocolate ______________________________ tasted delicious.   1 mark

4. First, ______________________________ the egg white from the yolk.   1 mark

5. The climbers made the ______________________________ successfully.   1 mark

6. The class watched the royal ______________________________.   1 mark

7. Ahmed is making ______________________________ progress.   1 mark

8. Phil is our ______________________________ monitor.   1 mark

9. Newton discovered the ______________________________ of gravity.   1 mark

10. The ______________________________ blew the candle out.   1 mark

End of Test! Now check your answers on p. 44!

1. Draw a line to connect each word to the correct **suffix** so that it makes an **adjective**.

Word **Suffix**

| malice | able |

| thought | ious |

| excite | ful |

1 mark

2. Use the **conjunctions** from the box below to complete the following sentence. You may use each conjunction only once.

| because | so | while |

_______________ I feel a lot healthier _______________ I am cycling to work now, I am

more tired in the evenings, _______________ I go to bed earlier.

1 mark

3. Draw a circle around the **subject** in the following sentence.

Last   Monday,   Boris   received   a   large   parcel   from   Jim,   his   cousin.

1 mark

4. Draw a line to connect each sentence to the correct **determiner**. You may use each determiner only once.

Sentence **Determiner**

| "Do you want ___ apple juice or orange juice?" | my |

| "I don't like ___ kind; I prefer cranberry." | either |

| "That's funny; ___ sister is exactly the same." | some |

1 mark

5. **Tick ONE BOX** to identify the option that must end with an **exclamation mark**.

What was the final score of the match ☐

That was a terrific match, wasn't it ☐

What an exciting match that was ☐

They said that it had been the most exciting match they'd ever seen ☐

1 mark

6. **Tick ONE BOX** to show which sentence uses the **semi-colon** correctly.

This election will be a close one there is no clear winner; according to the polls. ☐

This election will be a close one; there is no clear winner according to the polls. ☐

This election will be; a close one there is no clear winner according to the polls. ☐

This election; will be a close one there is no clear winner according to the polls. ☐

1 mark

7. Use an appropriate **adjective** to complete the following sentence.

The ______________________ artist's portraits were highly valued.

1 mark

8. **Tick ONE BOX** to show where the missing **inverted commas** should go in the sentence below.

☐   ☐   ☐   ☐

"Do you know when the submission deadline is? inquired Lydia.

1 mark

9. Put **one** dash in the correct place in the following sentence.

Gary stopped and stared in amazement he'd never seen such a huge cat!

1 mark

10. **Tick ONE BOX** in each row to show whether the sentence is in the **present perfect** or the **past perfect**.

SENTENCE	Present Perfect	Past Perfect
Rick has asked for a bicycle for his birthday.		
He had wanted a moped.		
However, his parents have refused to buy him one.		

1 mark

End of Test A! Now check your answers on p. 39!

1. Replace the underlined words in the sentence below with the correct **pronouns**.

Jack and Jill are terribly irresponsible: <u>Jack and Jill</u> were meant to be here by 10 o'clock, but we are still waiting for <u>Jack and Jill</u>.

1 mark

2. **Tick ONE BOX** to show which sentence uses the **colon** correctly.

These shorts come in four colours: dark grey, light blue, black and neon pink. ☐

These shorts come in four: colours dark grey, light blue, black and neon pink. ☐

These shorts come in four colours: dark grey: light blue: black and neon pink. ☐

These shorts: come in four colours dark grey, light blue, black and neon pink. ☐

1 mark

3. **Tick ONE BOX** to identify the sentence that shows Carlos is **most likely** to visit us next month.

Carlos may visit us next month. ☐

Carlos could visit us next month. ☐

Carlos might visit us next month. ☐

Carlos shall visit us next month. ☐

1 mark

4. Insert a **comma** in the correct place in the following sentence.

Although it was old and rusty Roger loved his grandfather's toolbox. *1 mark*

5. Draw a line to connect each sentence to its correct **function**. You may use each function only once.

Sentence	Function
How full of rubbish those bins are	statement
If they are full, empty the rubbish bins	question
Rubbish bins should be emptied regularly	exclamation
Those rubbish bins are still full, aren't they	command

1 mark

6. **Tick ONE BOX** to identify the sentence which is written in **Standard English**.

Mike thoughted about the problem long and hard. ☐

Horace and Omar been standing in the queue for two hours. ☐

Patty brought her laptop to work yesterday. ☐

Betsy drunk all her juice before she ate her sandwich. ☐

1 mark

7. Identify the punctuation marks on either side of the words <u>who had repeatedly lied</u> in the following sentence.

Jim — who had repeatedly lied — begged Nancy several times to forgive him.

____

1 mark

8. **Tick ONE BOX** to show which sentence uses **capital letters** correctly.

The national Health Service has recently celebrated its Seventieth Year. ☐

The national Health Service has recently celebrated its Seventieth year. ☐

The National Health Service has recently celebrated its seventieth year. ☐

The National Health service has recently celebrated its seventieth year. ☐

1 mark

9. In the passage below, circle the word that contains an **apostrophe** for **contraction**.

By the battle's end, it was clear the Russians had lost. No surprise, then, that the soldiers' morale was so low. As their opponents' cheers rang in their ears, each man thought it'd been a complete disaster.

1 mark

10. In the sentence below, circle all the **prepositions**.

Grace sighed contentedly as she sat beneath her favourite oak tree in her local park: it was a beautiful spring afternoon.

1 mark

End of Test B! Now check your answers on p. 40!

1. Using the boxes given, write the **expanded forms** of the underlined word or words in each of the following sentences.

Be gentle with those glasses; <u>they're</u> very fragile!

I <u>haven't</u> got any others so <u>you'll</u> have to be careful.

1 mark

2. Your teacher is helping you to correct the punctuation of the sentence in the following box. **Tick TWO BOXES** to show which pieces of advice you are given.

"Who goes there"? demanded, the sentry.

There should be speech marks after the word 'sentry', not the word 'there'. ☐

The question mark should be immediately after the word 'there'. ☐

There should be a question mark after the word 'sentry'. ☐

There should be a comma before the word 'demanded'. ☐

There shouldn't be a comma after the word 'demanded'. ☐

1 mark

3. **Tick ONE BOX** to show the meaning of the root <u>ped</u> in the word family below.

bi**ped**   **ped**al   centi**ped**e   **ped**estrian

walk ☐

many ☐

foot ☐

movement ☐

1 mark

4. **Tick ONE BOX** in each row to show if the use of the **comma** in the sentence is correct or incorrect.

SENTENCE	Correct	Incorrect
The saucepans, which were dirty had been left in the sink.		
The statue, a priceless Roman artefact, has been stolen.		
No matter how hard I begged, Diana refused to help me.		
Pete, Josh, Ravi, Ahmed, and Kyle all dislike yogurt.		

1 mark

5. Rearrange the words in the following statement to turn it into a **question**. Use the given words only. Make sure you punctuate your answer correctly.

Statement: All the sailors were wearing their uniforms.

Question: ____

1 mark

6. In the sentence below, circle the two words that show the **tense**.

For thirty years, Mr Thomas did precisely the same thing every morning — he made his wife a cup of tea.

1 mark

7. In each of the following sentences, underline the **main clause**.

Despite his many years of experience, Danny was not offered the job.

Andy sneezed violently when Fiona, his sister, spilt pepper everywhere.

Once they arrived, the police started to question the people who'd seen the accident.

1 mark

8. Circle the **conjunction** in each of the following sentences.

The customer won't leave until she is given a refund.

Rubin was pleased, for he'd managed to beat his own record.

1 mark

9. **Tick ONE BOX** in each row to show whether the clause in bold is a **main clause (M)** or a **subordinate clause (S)**.

SENTENCE	M	S
While they are good for you, you shouldn't eat too many tomatoes.		
I'm sitting in the back row and **Anna is sitting beside me**.		
Uncle Chris made a shocking announcement **as we were leaving**.		

1 mark

10. Circle the two **conjunctions** in the following sentence.

After Mark had walked all the way to the shops, he realised he'd left his wallet at home, so he had to go back for it.

1 mark

End of Test C! Now check your answers on p. 40!

1. Insert a **colon** in the correct place in the following sentence.

    Rhoda squealed suddenly she'd just seen a mouse!   1 mark

2. Underline the word that completes the following sentence correctly.

    Typically, sales of (stationery / stationary) increase at the beginning of term.   1 mark

3. Use the correct **possessive pronoun** to replace the underlined word or words in each of the
    following sentences.

    These paperweights belong to <u>Josh</u>. These paperweights are __________________.

    The house is owned by <u>Mr and Mrs Green</u>. The house is ________________.

    That book belongs to <u>my sister and me</u>. It is ________________.   1 mark

4. Explain the meaning of the word **synonym**.

    ____

    ____   1 mark

5. Write one word that is the **synonym** of the word <u>miserable</u>.

    ____   1 mark

6. Using **adverbs** derived from the adjectives in brackets, complete the following passage. One
    has been done for you.

    Tina ______**spitefully**______ [spiteful] broke her younger brother's favourite toy. When

    Ivan discovered this, he wept __________________ [bitter]. Their mother, Gina, was

    __________________ [understandable] furious with her daughter.   1 mark

22

7. How do the different **suffixes** change the meanings of the two following sentences?

Ali said that Polly felt quite <u>hopeful</u>.

This means that Polly ____

____

____

Ali said that Polly felt quite <u>hopeless</u>.

This means that Polly ____

____

____
1 mark

8. Rewrite the verbs in the boxes below using the **present progressive tense** to complete the sentences.

Neil _____________________ by the phone as he _____________________ anxiously

| sit | | wait |

for a call from his girlfriend.

Tod _____________________ about all the work he has to do.

| whinge |
1 mark

9. **Tick ONE BOX** to show which option completes the following sentence correctly.

" ________ been sleeping in my bed?" growled Papa Bear.

Whose   ☐

Whom   ☐

Who's   ☐

Which   ☐
1 mark

10. In the following sentence, underline the **relative clause**.

That house that is painted blue has just been sold to an Italian family.   1 mark

End of Test D! Now check your answers on p. 40!

1. Use the word <u>insult</u> as a **verb** in a sentence of your own. Do not change the word. Make sure you punctuate your sentence correctly.

____

1 mark

2. Use the word <u>insult</u> as a **noun** in a sentence of your own. Do not change the word. Make sure you punctuate your sentence correctly.

____

1 mark

3. **Tick ONE BOX** in each row to show if the sentence is written in the **active voice** or the **passive voice**.

SENTENCE	Active	Passive
Cotton has been grown in Egypt for centuries.		
It is famous for its long fibre which makes it softer and stronger.		
In the past, it has been called 'white gold'.		

1 mark

4. Rewrite the sentence below in the **passive voice**. Make sure you punctuate your answer correctly.

Millions of people are watching the World Cup.

____

1 mark

5. Circle each of the two **adjectives** in the sentence.

The   poor   ugly   duckling   cried   softly   to   himself   when   his   brothers   and

sisters   laughed   cruelly   at   him.

1 mark

6. Put one **colon** in the correct place in the following sentence.

Ravi   wants   to   become   a   botanist   a   person   who   studies   plants.

1 mark

7. **Tick ONE BOX** to show how the underlined words in the sentence below are used.

Later that day, Jorge realised what he'd forgotten to do in the morning.

a subordinate clause ☐

a fronted adverbial ☐

a noun phrase ☐

a relative clause ☐

1 mark

8. **Tick ONE BOX** to select the verb that completes the sentence in the **subjunctive form**.

It is vital that the headmaster _______ made aware of this.

were ☐

is ☐

are ☐

be ☐

1 mark

9. **Tick ONE BOX** to identify the function of the underlined words in the following sentence.

"I can't believe you've lost both pairs of sunglasses!" exclaimed Wilma.

a subordinate clause ☐

a preposition phrase ☐

a noun phrase ☐

a relative clause ☐

1 mark

10. **Tick ONE BOX** to show which sentence uses the **present perfect** form.

Felicity admitted that she had eaten all the chocolate cake. ☐

Pirates were lying in wait for the admiral's treasure ship. ☐

Since she started her new job, Rachel has been much happier. ☐

After the announcement was made, everyone began to make phone calls. ☐

1 mark

End of Test E! Now check your answers on p. 40!

1. Teresa works for a travel _________________________________.

    1 mark

2. The school _________________________________ sang beautifully.

    1 mark

3. Heba must not _________________________________ her mobile again.

    1 mark

4. The king's _________________________________ lasted twenty years.

    1 mark

5. The _________________________________ blew his whistle.

    1 mark

6. The tree's bark was _________________________________.

    1 mark

7. Sherif's pencil has a soft _________________________________.

    1 mark

8. Warm clothing is _________________________________ in winter.

    1 mark

9. There was _________________________________ among the politicians.

    1 mark

10. Demeter _________________________________ the loss of her daughter.

    1 mark

End of Test! Now check your answers on p. 44!

1. **Tick ONE BOX** to show which sentence should end with a **question mark**.

He didn't know how much it cost ☐

Ask Paul how much it costs ☐

How much did it cost ☐

Tell me how expensive it was ☐

1 mark

2. **Tick ONE BOX** to show which **pair of verbs** completes the sentence correctly.

In the fifteenth century, Leonardo da Vinci's flying machine _____ considered _____ revolutionary; now, however, the aeroplane is commonplace.

was   being   ☐

was   to be   ☐

were   to be   ☐

is   being   ☐

1 mark

3. **Tick ONE BOX** to show which sentence is correctly punctuated.

Completely exhausted, the climber finally reached the summit. ☐

Completely exhausted the climber finally reached, the summit. ☐

Completely exhausted the climber finally, reached the summit. ☐

Completely, exhausted the climber finally reached the summit. ☐

1 mark

4. **Tick ONE BOX** to show which sentence is in the **past tense**.

London Zoo is a popular tourist attraction. ☐

It houses almost 1000 different species. ☐

It is situated in Regent's Park in Central London. ☐

The zoo was intended to be used for scientific study. ☐

1 mark

5. Circle one word in each underlined pair to complete the sentences below in **Standard English**.

When I **come / came** in, I saw her.

She **was / were** wearing black trousers.

1 mark

6. Draw a line to match each **prefix** to the correct word so that it makes a new word.

Prefix	Word
sub	hear
dis	cast
non	miss
fore	sense
mis	stance

1 mark

7. In the box, write the **contracted form** of the underlined words.

I have decided that I <u>shall not</u> go to the gym tomorrow.

1 mark

8. **Tick ONE BOX** to show which sentence should end with an **exclamation mark**.

She asked me whether I was leaving ☐

You won't leave tomorrow, will you ☐

How rude of them to tell me to leave ☐

She was asked to leave the next day ☐

1 mark

9. **Tick ONE BOX** to show which sentence uses an **apostrophe** correctly.

Two rowdy players' names were taken down by the referees. ☐

Two rowdy player's names were taken down by the referees. ☐

Two rowdy players names' were taken down by the referees. ☐

Two rowdy players names were taken down by the referee's. ☐

1 mark

10. Circle all the **pronouns** in the following sentence.

As Tom was hungry, he poured himself a glass of milk and made himself two large cheese sandwiches with chutney and tomatoes in them.

1 mark

End of Test A! Now check your answers on p. 41!

1. **Tick ONE BOX** to show what the word <u>these</u> refers to in the following passage.

Our local museum is famous for its collections of Roman jewellery, weapons and mosaics. Many of <u>these</u> portray scenes from everyday life.

scenes ☐

collections ☐

mosaics ☐

weapons ☐

1 mark

2. Complete the following sentence with an **adjective** formed from the verb <u>talk</u>.

Mrs Lewis, who is over eighty, is an extremely _______________________________

person who loves telling stories about her past.

1 mark

3. **Tick ONE BOX** to show which part of the sentence is a **relative clause**.

At the top of the steep hill stands the house which is said to be haunted.

☐   ☐   ☐   ☐

1 mark

4. **Tick ONE BOX** to show **how** the underlined words are used in the sentence.

Unless everyone hurries up and gets in the car right now, <u>we'll be late</u>!

as a preposition phrase ☐

as a main clause ☐

as a noun phrase ☐

as a relative clause ☐

1 mark

5. Name the **punctuation mark** used between the two main clauses in the sentence below.

We agreed that Marie's party, which was last Friday evening, was a complete success: there wasn't a single complaint from anyone, even Martha!

____

1 mark

6. **Tick ONE BOX** in each row to show how the **modal verb** affects the meaning of each sentence.

SENTENCE	Certainty	Possibility
If you don't put on something warm, you might catch a cold.		
As Kelly's car has broken down, she will be late.		
Surprisingly, crocodiles can move very quickly.		
We could have cauliflower cheese for supper tonight.		

1 mark

7. **Tick ONE BOX** in each row to show whether the clause in bold is a **main clause (M)** or a **subordinate clause (S)**.

SENTENCE	M	S
Ants, **which live in colonies**, are found almost everywhere.		
Amazingly, in England alone, **there are over a hundred different species**.		
Although they can be annoying, **ants do help the environment**.		

1 mark

8. Circle **ALL** the **conjunctions** in the following sentences.

Whenever Tina goes to visit her grandfather, she always bakes him a chocolate cake, which is his favourite dessert.

Last week, Tina thought she would try something different and made him a carrot cake.

Although her grandfather was not very enthusiastic initially, after he had tried the carrot cake, he decided he liked it too.

1 mark

9. Circle the two words in the following sentence that are **synonyms**.

The frail old man slowly hobbled up the path, his feeble movements arousing pity among the sympathetic bystanders.

1 mark

10. **Tick ALL** the sentences that contain a **preposition**.

They couldn't see what lay beyond the hill. ☐

We left the theatre after the play had ended. ☐

He hasn't visited us since September. ☐

A bicycle knocked her over. ☐

1 mark

End of Test B! Now check your answers on p. 41!

1. Use the word <u>permit</u> as a **noun** in a sentence of your own. Do not change the word. Make sure you punctuate your sentence correctly.

____

1 mark

2. Use the word <u>permit</u> as a **verb** in a sentence of your own. Do not change the word. Make sure you punctuate your sentence correctly.

____

1 mark

3. **Tick ONE BOX** to show the meaning of the root <u>manu</u> in the word family below.

manuscript   manual   manufacture

to write	☐
by oneself	☐
by hand	☐
to create	☐

1 mark

4. Draw a line to match each word to its correct **antonym**.

Word	Antonym
surrender	expose
conceal	direct
curtail	elongate
serpentine	resistance

1 mark

5. Rewrite the following sentence, adding a **subordinate clause**. Remember to punctuate your sentence correctly.

Sita was watching a snooker match.

____

1 mark

6. Label the boxes below with **V (verb)**, **S (subject)** and **O (object)** to show the parts of the sentence.

While <u>Karim</u> <u>was waiting</u> for the doctor, the nurse took <u>his temperature</u>.

1 mark

7. Circle all the words in the sentences below that should start with a **capital letter**.

alexander the great was tutored by aristotle, the famous philosopher.

alexander became the ruler of macedonia when his father died.

1 mark

8. **Tick ONE BOX** to show which sentence is written in the **active voice**.

There were many brave soldiers in the army.

The library books were returned on time.

An emergency meeting was held in the town hall.

Three days ago, our neighbour's car was stolen.

1 mark

9. **Tick ONE BOX** to show which sentence is punctuated correctly.

She might come to the party — you never know with her but, I think it's highly unlikely.

She might come to the party, you never know with, her — but I think it's highly unlikely.

She might come to the party — you never know with her but — I think it's highly unlikely.

She might come to the party — you never know with her — but I think it's highly unlikely.

1 mark

10. **Tick ONE BOX** to show the correct place for a **semi-colon** in the sentence below.

The dinosaur skeleton was a hit at the museum the other exhibits were not as popular.

1 mark

End of Test C! Now check your answers on p. 41!

1.   **Tick ONE BOX** to show which sentence below uses the **present progressive**.

The deer were grazing in the glade. ☐

The rabbits have eaten all our carrots. ☐

The grasshoppers are making a terrible racket. ☐

We saw two robins building their nest in a plant pot. ☐

1 mark

2.   **Tick ONE BOX** to show which sentence below is a **command**.

I want everyone to come to the meeting. ☐

Don't be late tomorrow morning. ☐

You need to be here at 10 o'clock sharp. ☐

Everyone should bring a notebook and a pencil. ☐

1 mark

3.   Rewrite the following statement as **direct speech**. Remember to punctuate your answer correctly.

The zoo-keeper warned them not to give the monkeys nuts.

The zoo-keeper warned them, _______________________________________

____

1 mark

4.   Insert a pair of **brackets** in the correct place in the following sentence.

All   of   the   men   who   had   fought   so   valiantly   received   medals   from

the   king.

1 mark

5.   **Tick ONE BOX** in each row to show if the underlined word is an **adjective** or an **adverb**.

SENTENCE	Adjective	Adverb
We haven't been there <u>lately</u>.		
They were <u>hard</u> workers.		
I haven't seen him <u>before</u>.		
The man walked <u>very</u> slowly.		

1 mark

6. Complete the following sentence with an **adverb** formed from the adjective <u>responsible</u>.

Before they went out for the evening, Mr and Mrs Lee asked their children to behave

_________________________________.

<u>1 mark</u>

7. **Tick ONE BOX** to show which sentence below uses the **hyphen** correctly.

Mrs Brown always attends the end-of-term-party at school. ☐

Mrs Brown always attends the end-of-term party at school. ☐

Mrs Brown always attends the end of-term-party at school. ☐

Mrs Brown always attends the-end-of-term party at school. ☐ <u>1 mark</u>

8. Rewrite the following sentence in the **passive voice**. Punctuate your sentence correctly.

A loud noise woke her in the middle of the night.

____

<u>1 mark</u>

9. **Tick ONE BOX** in each row to show whether the word <u>since</u> is being used as a **preposition** or as a **subordinating conjunction**.

SENTENCE	Preposition	Subordinating conjunction
He has not been seen <u>since</u> 10 o'clock last night.		
My scarf's been missing <u>since</u> the rugby match at the weekend.		
Sadly, our team hasn't won a match <u>since</u> we beat Arsenal last season.		

<u>1 mark</u>

10. Complete the following sentence so that it uses the **subjunctive form**.

I suggest that he _______________________ harder to improve his technique. <u>1 mark</u>

End of Test D! Now check your answers on p. 41!

1. Complete the following table by adding a **suffix** to each noun to make an **adjective**.

Noun	Adjective
hunger	
euphoria	
emotion	
rage	
shine	

1 mark

2. **Tick ONE BOX** in each row to show whether the word in bold is a **subordinating conjunction** or a **co-ordinating conjunction**.

SENTENCE	Subordinating conjunction	Co-ordinating conjunction
If you work hard, they say, you will succeed.		
She practises regularly, **whereas** he doesn't.		
Their team won, **for** they trained all year.		

1 mark

3. Circle all the **determiners** in the following sentence.

There isn't much salt left, so you must buy some tomorrow.

1 mark

4. Write a sentence that lists all the information given in the following box. Remember to punctuate your answer correctly.

Things you need to make a rabbit hutch
ply wood
wire mesh
hinges
a bolt lock
screws

____

____

____

1 mark

5. Underline the longest possible **noun phrase** in the following sentence.

James, my friend, is hoping that he will get a role in our school play. 1 mark

6. Underline the **verb form** in the **present perfect** in the following passage.

Jake had thought that living in the countryside would be boring. However, since his family moved to their new cottage, he has made many new friends and spends hours exploring his new surroundings. 1 mark

7. Complete the following sentence with a **possessive pronoun**.

Those books belong to them; they are ________________________________. 1 mark

8. Circle the **adverb** in the following sentence.

After they had searched everywhere, they found their missing ball behind the garden shed. 1 mark

9. Insert a **colon** in the correct place in the following sentence.

Cats can be very lazy creatures sometimes, all they do is eat and sleep. 1 mark

10. Tick ONE BOX to show which **punctuation mark** should be in the place indicated by the arrow.

Leyton said, "There's no more milk" Jane had thought there was some left in the fridge.

↑

comma	☐
ellipsis	☐
full stop	☐
hyphen	☐

1 mark

End of Test E! Now check your answers on p. 42!

1. His opponent's _________________________ let Jeff score a goal.

    1 mark

2. Our bodies use _________________________ to build muscles.

    1 mark

3. Anna's house is _________________________ and well-furnished.

    1 mark

4. Ben's father is a _________________________ advisor.

    1 mark

5. Wanda _________________________ the deli on her way home.

    1 mark

6. Wellington _________________________ a plan to beat Napoleon.

    1 mark

7. Rose looked up the book in the _________________________.

    1 mark

8. The _________________________ flew down the hill.

    1 mark

9. Saul's handwriting is _________________________.

    1 mark

10. The dog guarded his master's _________________________.

    1 mark

Before using the Answers, please note the following:

MARKS
- In all the Grammar and Punctuation Tests, each **correct answer** is worth **1 mark**.
- Half marks **may not be awarded**.

MULTIPLE ANSWERS
- When a question requires **more than one answer**, **ALL** the student's given **responses must be correct** for their answer to be regarded as right. For example, if the correct answers are the words *his* and *him*, the student must provide <u>both</u> correct words.
- When a question can be **correctly answered in more than one way**, this is noted in this section and an **example** of at least **one possible correct** answer is given.

ADDITIONAL MARKING GUIDANCE
- Where necessary, additional marking guidance has been supplied in italics.

ANSWERS TO 'TICK BOX' QUESTIONS
- Where the student must show their chosen answer by ticking at least one box, this section gives the correct answer(s), followed by which box(es) should be ticked: *1st box, 2nd box, 3rd box, etc.*
  - For sets of vertical boxes, the topmost box is the 1st box, and so on.
  - For sets of horizontal boxes, the leftmost box is the 1st box, and so on.

ANSWERS

Group 4: Test A (pp. 5-6)

(1) How pretty she looked in that gown *(3rd box)*
(2) ...problem — work.
(3) Last Tuesday, at the theatre, we saw a Shakespeare play: *Hamlet. (2nd box)*
(4) twice a year *(4th box)*
(5) has organised *(2nd box)*
(6) doesn't; don't; don't

(7) As fast as possible, Raymond raced *(1st box)*
(8) I want to read a book, watch TV, listen to music and go swimming at the same time. *(4th box)*
(9) conjunction *(1st box)*
(10) ...doorbell <u>rang; we</u> all... *(2nd box)*

Group 4: Test B (pp. 7-8)

(1) verbs *(3rd box)*
(2) I like the idea of a hybrid: a car that uses both petrol and electricity. *(2nd box)*
(3) Doing it this way is like putting the cart <u>before</u> the horse. *(4th box)*
(4) Betty, much to her surprise, has won this month's competition. *(2nd box)*
(5) for
(6) Have you collected all your things from the hall *(3rd box)*

(7) <u>Clean</u> your teeth properly after every meal. *(1st box)*
(8) Yolanda travelled to a South Pacific island last year. *(1st box)*
(9) War <u>Horse, a</u> novel...War <u>I, has</u> been...
(10) the girls → they; the raincoats that belong to us → ours

(1) "Please, be quiet," said Gina, "because the baby's asleep." *(2nd box)*
(2) "Be on time for rugby practice, guys!" said the coach. *(4th box)*
(3) Millie grated the carrots and <u>Peter mashed the potatoes</u>. *(3rd box)*
(4) turbulent; tranquil
(5) Jade hid Fred's... → possession;
Where's the remote... → contraction;
Their dog's gone... → contraction;
Omar can't come... → contraction
(6) The clock that is on the mantelpiece is an antique. *(1st box)*
(7) He was asked to drive slowly *(2nd box)*
(8) ...our team<u>.</u> <u>He</u> didn't play...we lost<u>.</u>
We're hoping...next weekend<u>.</u>
(9) ...clothes — especially...Italy — are...
(10) to complete → completed; to begin → began **OR** had begun **OR** was begun

(1) *Answers will differ. Example:* To start with, switch on the washing machine.
(2) Saladin, the pure-bred Arabian, streaked ahead of the other horses → (M); he won the race easily → (M)
(3) because; yet; Once
(4) Rick passed an interesting-looking bookshop. *(1st box)*; The distant mountainous horizon was forbidding. *(3rd box)*
(5) Malcolm *(4th box)*
(6) <u>Helen,</u> my...<u>cousin,</u> enjoyed...<u>film;</u> she'd...
(7) theirs
(8) to be → was; to trip → tripped; to fall → fell
(9) ...sandwiches (<u>one</u> beef...<u>turkey</u>) as well...
(10) un- **OR** un

(1) perceptive; observant
(2) whose
(3) comma *(3rd box)*
(4) delightful; delightedly
(5) sufficient **OR** insufficient
(6) ...a <u>state-of-the-art</u> computer...
(7) *Answers will differ. Example:* The heavy rain has caused severe flooding.
(8) watched → were watching; were → were being
(9) *Answers will differ. Example:* Screaming loudly, <u>the cowardly knight</u> tried to escape...
(10) likely

(1) malice → ious; thought → ful; excite → able
(2) <u>While</u> I...healthier <u>because</u>...evenings, <u>so</u> I...
(3) Boris
(4) "Do you want ___ apple juice... → some;
"I don't like ___ kind... → either;
"That's funny; ___ sister... → my
(5) What an exciting match that was *(3rd box)*
(6) This election will be a close one; there is no clear winner according to the polls. *(2nd box)*
(7) *Answers will differ. Example:* talented.
(8) ...is? inquired... *(3rd box)*
(9) ...amazement — he'd...
(10) Rick has asked... → present perfect;
He had wanted... → past perfect;
...parents have refused... → present perfect

(1) <u>Jack and Jill</u> were → they; for <u>Jack and Jill</u> → them
(2) These shorts come in four colours: dark grey, light blue, black and neon pink. *(1st box)*
(3) Carlos shall visit us next month. *(4th box)*
(4) ...<u>rusty,</u> Roger...
(5) How full of rubbish... → exclamation;
If they are full... → command;
Rubbish bins should... → statement;
Those rubbish bins... → question
(6) Patty brought her laptop to work yesterday. *(3rd box)*
(7) dashes **OR** a pair of dashes
(8) The National Health Service has recently celebrated its seventieth year. *(3rd box)*
(9) it'd
(10) beneath; in

(1) they're → they are; haven't → have not; you'll → you will
(2) The question mark should be immediately after the word 'there'. *(2nd box)*; There shouldn't be a comma after the word 'demanded'. *(5th box)*
(3) foot *(3rd box)*
(4) The saucepans, which... → incorrect;
The statue, a priceless... → correct;
No matter how hard... → correct;
Pete, Josh, Ravi,... → incorrect
(5) Were all the sailors wearing their uniforms?
(6) did; made
(7) ...experience, <u>Danny was not offered the job</u>;
<u>Andy sneezed violently</u> when...;
...arrived, <u>the police started to question the people who'd seen the accident.</u>
(8) until; for
(9) While they are good for you... → (S);
...Anna is sitting beside me. → (M);
...as we were leaving. → (S)
(10) After; so

(1) ...squealed <u>suddenly:</u> she'd...
(2) stationery *(1st word)*
(3) his; theirs; ours
(4) *Answers will differ. Example:* A synonym is a word that has the same meaning as, or a similar meaning to, another word.
(5) *Answers will differ. Example:* depressed.
(6) bitterly; understandably
(7) *Answers will differ. Examples:* hopeful → had hope; hopeless → had no hope.
(8) sit → is sitting; wait → is waiting; whinge → is whingeing
(9) Who's *(3rd box)*
(10) <u>that is painted blue</u>

(1) *Answers will differ. Example:* I did not mean to <u>insult</u> you.
(2) *Answers will differ. Example:* We all gasped at the terrible <u>insult</u>.
(3) Cotton has been... → passive;
It is famous... → active;
In the past, it has been... → passive
(4) *Answers will differ. Example:* The World Cup is being watched.
(5) poor; ugly
(6) ...<u>botanist:</u> a person...
(7) a fronted adverbial *(2nd box)*
(8) be *(4th box)*
(9) a noun phrase *(3rd box)*
(10) Since she started her new job, Rachel has been much happier. *(3rd box)*

(1) How much did it cost *(3rd box)*
(2) was to be *(2nd box)*
(3) Completely exhausted, the climber finally reached the summit. *(1st box)*
(4) The zoo was intended to be used for scientific study. *(4th box)*
(5) came; was
(6) sub → stance; dis → miss; non → sense;
fore → cast; mis → hear
(7) shall not → shan't
(8) How rude of them to tell me to leave *(3rd box)*
(9) Two rowdy players' names were taken down by the referees. *(1st box)*
(10) he; himself; himself; them

(1) mosaics *(3rd box)*
(2) talkative
(3) which is said to be haunted *(4th box)*
(4) as a main clause *(2nd box)*
(5) colon **OR** a colon
(6) ...you might catch... → possibility; ...she will be... → certainty; ...crocodiles can... → certainty; We could have... → possibility
(7) which live in colonies → S; there are over a hundred different species → M; ants do help the environment → M
(8) Whenever; and; Although; after
(9) frail; feeble
(10) They couldn't see what lay beyond the hill. *(1st box)*; He hasn't visited us since September. *(3rd box)*

(1) *Answers will differ. Example:* My parking permit has expired.
(2) *Answers will differ. Example:* The teacher will not permit us to do that.
(3) by hand *(3rd box)*
(4) surrender → resistance; conceal → expose; curtail → elongate; serpentine → direct
(5) *Answers will differ. Example:* Sita, who is very enthusiastic about sport, was watching a snooker match.
(6) Karim → S; was waiting → V; his temperature → O
(7) alexander; great; aristotle; alexander; macedonia
(8) There were many brave soldiers in the army. *(1st box)*
(9) She might come to the party — you never know with her — but I think it's highly unlikely. *(4th box)*
(10) ...museum; the... *(3rd box)*

(1) The grasshoppers are making a terrible racket. *(3rd box)*
(2) Don't be late tomorrow morning. *(2nd box)*
(3) *Answers may differ. Example:* The zoo-keeper warned them, "Do not give the monkeys nuts."
(4) ...men (who...valiantly) received...
(5) ...there lately → adverb; ...hard workers → adjective; ...him before → adverb; ...very slowly → adverb
(6) responsibly
(7) Mrs Brown always attends the end-of-term party at school. *(2nd box)*
(8) *Answers will differ. Example:* She was woken by a loud noise.
(9) ...seen since 10 o'clock... → preposition; ...missing since the... → preposition; ...match since we... → subordinating conjunction
(10) *Answers will differ. Example:* practise.

(1) hunger → hungry; euphoria → euphoric; emotion → emotional; rage → raging; shine → shiny

(2) If → subordinating conjunction; whereas → subordinating conjunction; for → co-ordinating conjunction

(3) much; some

(4) *Answers will differ. Example:* To make a rabbit hutch, you will need the following things: ply wood, wire mesh, hinges, a bolt lock and screws.

(5) <u>a role in our school play</u>

(6) has made

(7) theirs

(8) everywhere

(9) ...lazy <u>creatures</u>: sometimes, all...

(10) full stop *(3rd box)*

ADMINISTERING & MARKING THE SPELLING TESTS

ADMINISTERING THE SPELLING TESTS

- The **Spelling Tests** in this book **need to be read out loud** to the student from **the transcripts** provided in the following pages.

- Each spelling test in this book should take around 10 minutes.

- Before administering each spelling test, read out the following instructions.

  * *Listen carefully to these instructions.*
  * *There are 10 sentences in your test paper. Each sentence has a word missing from it.*
  * *I will first read the missing word on its own. Then, I will read the whole sentence with the missing word in it. Finally, I will read the missing word again on its own.*
  * *I will do this each time for each sentence.*
  * *Listen carefully to the missing word and write it in the space provided in your test paper.*
  * *Make sure you spell the word correctly.*

- Answer any questions the student may have before proceeding with the test.

- In the Transcripts, there are entries such as the one below:

  *Spelling 1: The word is **delighted**.*
  *Sam was **delighted** with his present.*
  *The word is **delighted**.*

- These should be read out to the student in the following manner:

  * *Read out loud "Spelling number 1."*
  * *Read out loud "The word is delighted."*
  * *Read out loud "Sam was delighted with his present."*
  * *Read out loud "The word is delighted."*

- Leave a gap of at least 12 seconds between each spelling.
- At the end, read all 10 sentences out again in order from the beginning.
- Give the student time to change any of their answers if they wish.
- When the test is over, say "This is the end of the test."

MARKING THE SPELLING TESTS

- Each **correctly spelt word** is worth **1 mark**.
- Half marks **are not to be awarded**.
- If a word requires a **capital letter, an apostrophe**, or **a hyphen**, these punctuation marks **must be used correctly** by the student **for the mark to be awarded**.
- Spellings that have been written as **two distinct** or **incorrectly hyphenated** words **cannot be accepted**.

GROUP 4: SPELLING TEST (P. 15)

Spelling 1: The word is **ceiling.**
A large crack appeared in the **ceiling.**
The word is **ceiling.**

Spelling 2: The word is **guessed.**
Bella **guessed** the right answer.
The word is **guessed.**

Spelling 3: The word is **dessert.**
The chocolate **dessert** tasted delicious.
The word is **dessert.**

Spelling 4: The word is **separate.**
First, **separate** the egg white from the yolk.
The word is **separate.**

Spelling 5: The word is **ascent.**
The climbers made the **ascent** successfully.
The word is **ascent.**

Spelling 6: The word is **procession.**
The class watched the royal **procession.**
The word is **procession.**

Spelling 7: The word is **noticeable.**
Ahmed is making **noticeable** progress.
The word is **noticeable.**

Spelling 8: The word is **stationery.**
Phil is our **stationery** monitor.
The word is **stationery.**

Spelling 9: The word is **principle.**
Newton discovered the **principle** of gravity.
The word is **principle.**

Spelling 10: The word is **draught.**
The **draught** blew the candle out.
The word is **draught.**

GROUP 5: SPELLING TEST (P. 26)

Spelling 1: The word is **agency.**
Teresa works for a travel **agency.**
The word is **agency.**

Spelling 2: The word is **choir.**
The school **choir** sang beautifully.
The word is **choir.**

Spelling 3: The word is **lose.**
Heba must not **lose** her mobile again.
The word is **lose.**

Spelling 4: The word is **reign.**
The king's **reign** lasted twenty years.
The word is **reign.**

Spelling 5: The word is **referee.**
The **referee** blew his whistle.
The word is **referee.**

Spelling 6: The word is **rough.**
The tree's bark was **rough.**
The word is **rough.**

Spelling 7: The word is **lead.**
Sherif's pencil has a soft **lead.**
The word is **lead.**

Spelling 8: The word is **essential.**
Warm clothing is **essential** in winter.
The word is **essential.**

Spelling 9: The word is **dissent.**
There was **dissent** among the politicians.
The word is **dissent.**

Spelling 10: The word is **mourned.**
Demeter **mourned** the loss of her daughter.
The word is **mourned.**

Spelling 1: The word is **hesitancy.**
His opponent's **hesitancy** let Jeff score a goal.
The word is **hesitancy.**

Spelling 2: The word is **protein.**
Our bodies use **protein** to build muscles.
The word is **protein.**

Spelling 3: The word is **spacious.**
Anna's house is **spacious** and well-furnished.
The word is **spacious.**

Spelling 4: The word is **financial.**
Ben's father is a **financial** advisor.
The word is **financial.**

Spelling 5: The word is **passed.**
Wanda **passed** the deli on her way home.
The word is **passed.**

Spelling 6: The word is **devised.**
Wellington **devised** a plan to beat Napoleon.
The word is **devised.**

Spelling 7: The word is **catalogue.**
Rose looked up the book in the **catalogue.**
The word is **catalogue.**

Spelling 8: The word is **sleigh.**
The **sleigh** flew down the hill.
The word is **sleigh.**

Spelling 9: The word is **illegible.**
Saul's handwriting is **illegible.**
The word is **illegible.**

Spelling 10: The word is **possessions.**
The dog guarded his master's **possessions.**
The word is **possessions.**